My thoughts and opinions
Eccedentesiast 7:17
(ex-ce-den-tee-see-est)

No, that is not a Bible verse.
That's a noun and a date,
made to look like a Bible verse to the
untrained eye.

Dedicated to the reader…
If you are reading this,
then you are going through a hard time
right now.
These pages come from my social media,
What I have posted and what are in my
drafts.
They are composed of my thoughts,
opinions, and poetry
about Love, Depression, Anxiety, Fear,
Peace, and Mental Health.
Some pages might be a personal matter,
while others are directed to a certain
audience.
These pages might become too real for
some,
And become too much for others.
Read at your discretion.
Enjoy…

Eccedentesiast- (.n) Someone who hides pain behind a smile.
(ex-ce-den-tee-see-est)

I believe that takes more strength than lifting weights.
Being in pain but still making jokes and having a smile on.
That's real strength.

11-22-20

There is a difference between having
time,
And making time.
And it's messed up if you make time for
someone,
But they don't have time for you.

7-17-20

I hate "imy" and "ily."
You miss or love me enough to type 3
letters
But you don't miss or love me enough to
type 5 more letters.
If you won't type 3 words to me,
Then you don't miss/ love me,
And just don't bother texting those
letters.

7-17-20

I have a plan for everything,
I have a backup plan for everything,
Sometimes I have a backup backup plan.
I have the main plan, one if it goes south,
One if it doesn't work or happen,
And I know what I need to do if there's a
flaw.
I have everything planned out.
Don't worry about me,
I have a plan.

12-18-20

Beauty is in the eye of the beholder;
Beauty lies even in chaos.
To everyone else
It looks like a jumbled mess,
But to you,
You see something breathtaking.
So, you love it.
And wonder how nobody else can see its
beauty.
Music, Art, Writing, Movies, People,
It never ends.

-draft

I can recall every time something inside
me broke
And changed how I think, see, and
behave around people.
7th, 10th, 12th, freshmen, sophomore year.
Each year had something different.
I don't want to make that list longer.
I only know 2 ways to fix that.
One takes time,
While the other is short and permanent.

-draft

Sometimes I get this dark feeling in my chest
And in my stomach.
I get them when I know what needs to happen to me,
And I realize that I've overstayed my welcome.

-draft

Falling is terrifying,
Especially if you don't have something to
catch you.
Falling out of a plane,
Falling off a swing,
Falling in love,
The fall of man.
We're terrified of these
Because we don't know if we'll be caught
Or if we will have something to catch us.

-draft

Every time I get a Snapchat
Or a text from someone I normally don't
get one from,
I won't answer or look at it for a few
hours.
What's going on in my mind is
What did I do?
What do they need from me?
Most of the time it's something negative
I think about,
Rarely it's something good.

I've been so accustomed to getting bad
news
From someone I don't normally talk to
Or them asking for something
That my mind jumps to it when
Their name pops up in my notifications.
I can't see snaps until I open it,
And I panic when it's a text.

-draft

I lost my mask.
Not the one for COVID,
But the other one.
The one I hide behind,
The one I wear in public
In front of my friends, my family, and
colleagues.
I lost it, and I don't know where it is.
Hopefully, it's not broken
Or I don't know what I'll do.
I lost my mask.

-draft

I was with my brother-in-law's family for
Christmas this year.
When we were opening presents,
I was looking at everyone
And realized I had never felt so alone.
Despite being surrounded by people,
I barely knew them.
I wish I had someone come with me to it.
Maybe then I wouldn't have felt so alone.

-draft

When I was in high school,
We had a school shooter threat from a
student.
I was in a group chat with people saying
they loved everyone.
The next day,
Half the school was gone.
I went to school that day.
After that experience I always had a fear
it would happen,
And I would get caught in the cross fire.

I ran these scenarios in my head,
About what my last words would be.
"Thank you."
Or
"Why me?"

-draft

I've learned that keeping my hands
And my mind busy,
Pauses my thoughts and my actions.
Listening to music,
Playing with Legos,
Playing music,
Playing video games,
Writing these,
Playing with dogs,
Etc.
These things are my safety plan.
So, if I do these,
Then I'm hurting bad,
And I hope I don't do anything bad.

-draft

I need to learn how to let go.
I know I'll feel better when I let go,
But,
I also know people might be hurt that I
did let go.
I don't know how long they will hurt
But I do know they will heal from it,
And I hope they forgive me for letting
go.
Let go of everything you fear to lose.
I need to learn how to let go.

-draft

I have some bad habits,
And some bad addictions.
I've noticed over the past few years,
I only have one bad habit at a time.
I trade one for another.
I'm trying to get rid of this habit
That I currently have,
And trade it for one I used to have.
Trying to get the lesser of 2 evils.

-draft

Dear God,
Thank you for letting me get all these
new connections and opportunities in my
life,
But I think it would be better if it was for
someone else.
Those weren't for me,
I wasn't supposed to make it this far,
So, it would be great to come home,
And see you.
Amen.

12-14-20

"You're not afraid to let go.
You're afraid that when you do,
Nothing is going to happen,
Nothing is going to change,
That everything will stay the same."
I said that in front of my parents,
And that is one of the things
that really spoke to my dad.

10-12-20

Every scar on my body didn't come from
a stranger.
They didn't come from family or friends
either.
It came from the one person
Who has been with me since the
beginning,
Who knows my demons,
And my angels.
They know everything about me.
Their name starts with the letter     M,
And ends with the letter               E.

-draft

I'm insecure about my body.
I'm also insecure about my hair,
How I walk, talk, eat, spell, read,
My handwriting,
Whether I'm annoying you or not,
How I smell, my teeth, my face,
What you think of me, and so much
more.
But I'm most insecure about the scars I
gave myself,
Especially the ones where everyone can
see.

11-22-20

I am a hypocrite.
Not "don't tell me what to do"
But the advice I give.
I've said some really great stuff.
But I don't take my own advice.
I said to be kind to yourself,
But look at what I've done to myself.
I am a hypocrite.

12-26-20

I am so broken, hurt, and tired.
But I have a heart of a child.
So, that means I do goofy things
like jump on leaves and build Legos.
And because I have a heart of a child,
I hand out my love like I'm not broken,
hurt, and tired.
I do that because I want people to feel
how I wish I felt;
Happy and loved.

11-22-20

Don't say you miss me
If you aren't going to call or FaceTime
me.
You miss me enough to text "I miss you"
But you don't miss me enough to call/
FaceTime me.
I don't care if you say I miss you because
I won't believe it,
You need to show it,
You miss me by calling me.

7-18-20

Behind every scar there is a story.
Good, bad,
Smart, dumb.
Behind my scars there are stories.
Most of them are the same story,
Just told from a different time,
Perspective,
And angle.
But the plot behind them
Are the same.
I know which of my scars have stories.

-draft

I don't know who the man in the mirror
is,
But I don't like him.
People call his name,
So that must be the man in the mirror's
name.
He's not me
And that's not my name,
So then the question is,
Who is he?

-draft

I'm at the end of something.
What that is I do not know
But I can feel the end of it coming.
Maybe it's something good
That is going to suck when it ends,
Or maybe it is something bad
That is going to rock when it ends.
I do not know.
But I do know something is ending.

-draft

People blame themselves for things
That weren't their fault.
Those weren't you're actions
So stop blaming yourself,
Stop saying you could've stopped it.

-draft

I believe most people deserve 2$^{nd}$ chances.
Not immediately
But in time.
Both of you will change in that time,
And when you two meet face to face,
Only then will you be able to decide
If they deserve a 2$^{nd}$ chance
Or not.

-draft

I just want to be able to close my eyes
And feel alright.

-draft

Any time I say "what makes you say
that?"
Means I want to know why you said that,
And want to come up with an answer
Around your answer.
I might get around you
By not saying everything,
Or I might let you find everything out.
What makes you say that?

-draft

My heart is stronger than my mind.
It can't do math
But it can make me feel like a superhero
When I see that one person.
It also knows who's bad for me
Before my mind figures it out.
I hate my heart sometimes,
But it still keeps me grounded here.

-draft

My demons are starting to haunt my
dreams.
First it was someone from high school,
Now it's someone from middle school.
These people, I don't talk to them
anymore.
I haven't seen in years.
And it's been happening for the past few
days

12-21-20

There's a difference between happiness,
And inner peace.
Happiness come from something
Or someone,
With joy and smiles appearing.
While inner peace is being content with
Who,
What,
And where you are.

I've been trying to be happy on my own
for a while,
Not trying to have someone be my source
of happiness.
I've been trying to find happiness in
myself,
But I think I need to find inner peace
first.

-draft

My heart and mind are still at war,
But my body and mind aren't.
They aren't synced with each other,
My body just gave up,
And my mind took over.

-draft

I'm scared that I will make it through this
by myself.
Becoming happy on my own
Without anyone's help.
If I do make it,
I just proved to myself
That I don't need anyone,
And I can pick myself up.
Don't be surprised if I don't talk about
myself anymore.
I know how to handle it.

-draft

If I ruin my relationships,
That means I'm trying to see if my heart
will fail
And my mind can slip past it.
If my mind can slip past my heart,
Then I may be able to do the thing
That lets me go from here.

Another meaning for that is
Self-sabotage.
It's a different form of self-harm
That not everyone can see.

-draft

I wish I didn't love so hard.
I feel like my life would be so much
easier.
But I do love hard,
I love people more than I love myself
Which is why I'm still here.
I don't want to be here
But my heart keeps me anchored.
I wish there was another me
To love me.
I wish I didn't love so hard.

-draft

It's appropriate to have a child-like heart
When you were a child.
To find someone with a childlike heart as
an adult
Is rare.
The best memories one can have as an
adult
Is by doing those child-like activities,
Preferably with someone else.

-draft

I wish I could remove who follows me.
Because this stuff is very personal,
And not openly like me.
I don't mind if strangers see them
Or people who knew me can see them
Because I know they'll do nothing about
it.
But the people whom I see and talk to
can.
And it scares me what they might do.

-draft

I was helping someone who looked at my
cuts on my hands
And wrists and said to me,
"Be kind to yourself."
He doesn't know how upset I am,
Cause he has no idea what's going on
with me,
And I prefer if people keep their
comments about my cuts
To themselves.
I'm still here,
And you don't know me.

-draft

I have out of body experiences.
Not like seeing myself in 3<sup>rd</sup> person,
But questioning everything.
How am I here,
Why am I here,
How am I seeing with my eyes,
How do I feel,
What happened before and after me,
Am I being controlled,
How am I doing all this.

And I panic for a short time,
Wide eyes,
Hand on my head,
But after that,
I'm fine.
Or I'm not questioning things anymore.
It's scary because
When I have those,

All these thoughts go through my head
And I become stuck,
I just think that some things
Are impossible with these questions.

-draft

I keep thinking back
To when my sister kicked me out over
quarantine
And my parents let her.
I had to live on my own.
She did get me food twice and let me do
laundry,
But she still kicked me out.
Now that I'm living with her again,
I'm in constant fear it's going to happen
again.

12-21-20

After a while it stops hurting.
Either it has healed,
Or you became numb to it.
This is for both the good and bad.
It no longer hurts when you say goodbye,
It no longer hurts when I get a new
wound.
It only hurts when it's in a new area,
That was originally untouched

12-19-20

I don't care what you say,
Words mean nothing to me.
If you want me to believe you then show
it.
I miss you, call me.
I love you, kiss me.
I hate you, beat me up.
If you say it but don't show it,
Then do you really mean what you say?
I only care about actions.

7-18-20

If you tell someone to not do something
Whether it's good or bad,
Why aren't you physically stopping
them?
Don't eat that cake,
Take the cake away from them.
Stop starving yourself,
Sit down with them and eat a meal.
Cause if you tell me to stop something,
Are you going to stop me?

7-21-20

One of my greatest fears is being
successful.
Having everything I've ever wanted,
Having a wife, dog, kids,
Being genuinely happy,
A nice house,
A successful career.
It's scary because,
Those things are foreign to me.
If I get those,
I'll panic.

-draft

My heart is the only thing keeping me
here.
Knowing my parents would cry,
And that I wouldn't see my dog again.
That's it.
Not even my siblings are part of it.
I know they will cry,
Or might cry.
My family doesn't feel like my family
anymore.

-draft

People ask me if I want a girlfriend,
It's not that I don't want one,
It's just 2 major flaws comes up.
    1.)    I don't want another earthly
        attachment.
    2.)    She needs to like me back.
Number 2 is the biggest reason why I
don't have one.

-draft

If you're going to fall in love with me,
Please fall in love with my actions.
Don't fall for my words
Or how I say them
Because words can be deceiving,
But actions speak true.
I'll rarely say "I Love You"
But my actions show that I Love You.

-draft

I do and say everything on purpose
And with multiple meanings.
If I do or say something,
I know exactly every reason why.
But some funny stuff I do,
I know it's funny,
I just don't know the psychology behind
why
It's funny.

-draft

I don't give up often,
But when I do
That means I believe there is no future
for it.
It doesn't matter if it's someone
Or something,
I will keep fighting
Till I can't fight anymore
And when I believe there is no future.

If I give up on someone,
I will try so hard to keep fighting,
But then I will stop talking
Till they talk to me first
Because I was always the one
Starting conversations.
So, I stopped,
And after awhile
If you don't say anything,
I'll give up on you.

-draft

There's a lot of bad in this world,
But at the same time
There's also a lot of good.
Stop looking for the bad
Or you'll never find good.
It's like a word search,
If you look for a specific word,
Then you'll skip over the other words on
the list,
Trying to find that one word.

Without the bad
You never know what's good.
It needs to be balanced.
If you take away all the bad,
It will become a chaotic good world.
The things we once saw as good,
Will start to look bad.

-draft

The heart only knows how to love.
It's the mind that plays games.
Sometimes your heart
And mind are at war with each other,
Fighting what you feel
Vs. what you know.
It's up to you to decide which is stronger,
Your heart,
Or your mind.

-draft

You think my posts are hard pills to
swallow.
You haven't seen my drafts.
There are more saved thoughts
And more harder pills to swallow.

-draft

If I could go back,
I would do everything sooner,
Both good
And bad.

-draft

We don't know anybody's real intentions
with us.
We can assume why they did that,
We can assume the reasons they did it,
But if we don't ask,
We won't know.
One simple way to see
Is to ask "Why?"
Why did you say or do XYZ?
Only then will you get your answer
And know their intentions.
If someone asks me to go somewhere
with them,
A million thoughts go through my head.
What do they need from me?
Who put them up to this?
Why would they want me to come with
them?
What's my backup plan?
Are they playing me?
But I don't know.

-draft

People say they love me and care about
me,
But I don't feel loved and cared for.
Being told that is good,
But being showed that is better.
Being shown that you're loved and cared
for
Will make me believe it.
I don't care what you say,
Just show it,
And I'll know.

10-4-20

If I open up and tell you my demons,
These thoughts in my mind,
It says at least 2 things.
  1.) How little you actually know
me.
  2.) How strong I actually am.

9-31-20

I am a fighter.
Maybe not on the outside,
But if you were in my shoes,
You would collapse with what I'm
carrying.
Now do that,
Put a smile on,
And say some jokes.
You would see how strong I really am
And how much I fight every day.

-draft

I don't want to die,
I just want the pain to stop.
But the pain is so intense
That I want a solution
To be just as intense.
Because the solution won't be as intense
I say no thank you
And go back into the fire.

Having this pain
Is like having your domino line fall
prematurely.
You have no idea what to do
Because it's all so fast
And so intense,
But the solution to making it stop
Is to remove a domino that's still
standing.
By removing the domino
It will make the line stop falling.

The destruction left was intense
And devastating

But the solution was simple and easy.
You didn't need to kick the line
To make it stop
But you would have preferred that
Because it was just as intense
As the destruction.
Keep your eyes open
And look for the domino to make it stop.

-draft

I hate when I'm with people
And I just get sad all of the sudden.
When I mentally feel alone,
Want to die,
Want to cut myself again,
Anything to make it stop.
Maybe I'm not supposed to be happy,
Maybe I'm supposed to suffer.
Or maybe I'm just so used to it
That I don't want to be happy.

-draft

I try to see the bright side of everything,
Getting a plus even out of something
bad.
That plus might be good for me
But bad for you.
Get a dog, good.
Lose a relationship, bad.
I try to look at what I've gained from it
Even if you see it as bad.

-draft

The sad thing about me is
I know how to love others,
I know how to make them laugh,
But I don't know how to love myself
Or how to make myself laugh.
And I'm not used to love and affection
So if I'm shown those,
I have a panic attack
Because they're so foreign to me.

-draft

The big difference between you and me
Is that you can walk away anytime you
want,
But I have to stay.
If you're mad at me you can leave,
But if I'm mad at myself,
I have to stay with the person I hate,
And it's exhausting.

10-22-20

I know you'll leave me,
And that's okay.
I knew you were going to leave me.
I hurt myself before you hurt me.

-draft

Being sad is so much easier
And truer than being happy.
You can fake a smile
And fake being happy,
But you can never fake a frown,
Or fake being sad.

-draft

I'm waiting for the day
When I can look at myself in the mirror,
And see myself
Not a stranger
And genuinely smile.
Say "hello old friend"
And be happy with who I am.

-draft

I date to marry,
But I also date so I can know
That I am capable
Of being loved in that way.

-draft

I've been doing this for God knows how long.
I honestly don't know how much more I can take.

-draft

Love surrounds all of us
Whether we want it to or not.


Love is the most addicting
And powerful drug that you can't buy.
Love can build you up
And break you down to and from
nothing.
Love can push you away
Or bring you back home.
The most kind hearted people love the
hardest.


The most broken person gives love to
everybody.
Love can turn this frown upside down.
Love can make the depressed have hope
And a future.

Love is not a physical thing that you can
touch
Or see,
It's felt with the heart.

-draft

If I ask you if you want to come with me
somewhere,
It's not so we can hook up.
It's so I have someone to talk to while
driving,
Eating,
And get to watch a movie
Or sing with.
But mainly it's a safety precaution for me,
So I don't do anything I may regret.

-draft

I don't like holidays,
Not like how grinch hates Christmas,
But because the magic from when I was
younger is gone.
I'm not excited anymore,
I spend them alone,
It's just another day, and boring.
This includes Christmas and my
birthday.
So, I don't really celebrate them anymore.

10-31-20

Someone asked me why I post these.
Not just because I'm sad.
These are my thought that I don't get to
say.
It's a place of my quotes.
A timeline of when I become
better/worse.
And so you can understand me,
Who I am, what I hide from people,
And what you're getting into.

11-9-20

Thank you past me
For fighting for so long and for staying
so strong.
You've been doing this for so long,
You must be so tired, and you need to let
go.
Let go.
It's time to go home.
You can't hold on forever.

11-9-20

I hate myself
But not others.
Which is why I suffer
Instead of ending it.
My heart won't let me end it,
So I try to break it
Hoping I'm able to leave.
I can get so close,
One more step,
But my heart won't let go.
So I suffer
Instead of ending it.

-draft

There's only 4 people I want to annoy.
My mom, dad,
Dog and future wife.
My mom and dad raised me
So they shouldn't be surprised.
My dog is my best friend.
My wife married me
So it's my job.

-draft

I do and say everything on purpose and
with multiple meanings,
So even the silliest or smallest thing I
do/say,
I put thought into it.
If you ask me why I did/say or didn't
do/say that,
The answer can be a very simple,
Or a very complex one.

11-9-20

The other night I woke up with my arms
hurting,
They weren't bleeding or anything,
But I had to keep them moving
Or they'll start to hurt again,
And feel like they're on fire.

-draft

I'm ready,
Not for everything
But some certain stuff.
I'm ready for both good and bad.
I'm ready to become happy,
For my sister to kick me out again,
To take a warm long shower,
To see God.

But there's also stuff I'm not ready for
Both good and bad.
I'm not ready to live on my own again,
To have someone who genuinely cares
about me,
To get old,
To confront my problems and trauma.

-draft

Sticks and stones can break your bones,
But words can break your heart.
Words can hurt and they do,
It takes your world and breaks it apart.

11-18-20

You can't take back what you said/did.
The damage is already done.
Whether it was to yourself or to others.
You can try to make it better,
But in doing so you might make it worse.

11-22-20

I hate goodbyes.
Even if they're 100 yards away.
Because you never know
If that's going to be the last "goodbye"
you'll ever give them.
You might still text,
But it's been years since you've seen them
in person.

11-22-20

In high school
I couldn't see myself after graduating.
That happened junior and senior year,
But now it's happening again in college.

-draft

I'm tired of being right all the time.
Not like the answer is "D,"
But with people's intentions
And me.

-draft

Everyone's will to live
Is still there,
They just have to find it.
It may be small,
But you will find it again.
You've lost it,
But in reality,
You just need to look in a different spot.
Once you find it,
You will also find yourself,
Or once you find yourself,
You will find it.

My will to live is lost in my childhood,
When I was happy,
Hopeful,
And joyful.
I know where it is,
I just don't know how to get to it,
So I'm lost.
Hopefully, I find it soon,
And hopefully by myself.

And if I don't,
Don't be mad or sad,
Just look up,
Smile,
And say goodbye.

-draft

I know I'm not the main character in my story,
I'm that side character that was cut from the finale film.

7-22-20

Right now,
I just want someone to hold me
While I break down
And just tell me I'm not worthless or to
sing to me.
But I know that's too much to ask for,
So can I get a text saying that.
Wait, that's also too much to ask for.

8-9-20

I realized I loved you
When you were the last thing I think of
Before falling asleep,
The first thing I think of
When I wake up,
And the only thing that hasn't left my mind
Since I first saw you.

-draft

I am a room.
At first glance it looks clean.
But take a closer look,
You can see how dirty it really is.

-draft

I yield, you win.

-draft

Sometimes I wonder
If people are wondering about me,
Or if I'm on anyone's mind.
I appreciate checkups,
But it means a whole lot if it's from the person
I was thinking about.
But I know the person I'm thinking of
Will never check up on me
Unless I check-up first.
And it hurts.

8-29-20

I'm not the type of person who will give
up on someone,
But I am the type of person who will give
up on myself
Mentally and physically for you.
Just look at me from a year ago
And remember who I was.
Remember how much I changed
But despite that,
I still helped you.

10-4-20

With the right person
5 hours can feel like 5 minutes.
When I'm with that person,
My mind doesn't know what to say,
So,
I speak nonsense or nothing.

-draft

Dear God,
I'm ready to come home now,
I think I've made an impact on this earth.
I've overstayed my welcome
And I'm ready to see you.
Amen.

10-22-20

I always get yelled at by my family.
Saying negative things that I am
& I believe them;
Lazy, annoying, my brother, my dad.
And other things they probably thought;
Slow, disappointment, disrespectful,
mistake.
For once I want someone to tell me
They're proud of the one thing I'm not.
Dead.

12-19-20

I am in a well right now.
At the bottom.
And the only way I'm getting out
Is if someone throws a ladder down
And helps me out,
Or if a hurricane comes
And fills the well with water.
I will struggle to survive and if I do,
Come out with scars.
But I may or may not survive it.

8-9-20

Nobody wants me,
Not even death wants me.

-draft

If you're able to leave,
am I able to leave?

-draft

I don't want someone to be my source of
happiness.
I want them to add on to it.
I know what will happen if they become
my source,
And it's not good.

-draft

The worst part about right now,
Is that my parents don't know how much
I'm hurting.
They questioned when my sister-in-law
Stayed in her room all day
But not me.
They just think I'm lazy,
When I'm really exhausted.

8-9-20

I know I'm a lot to deal with and handle,
So if you're still with me
And for me,
Thank you.
I know at times I can be annoying
And be difficult.
I like to say it's worth it in the end
Because my love and loyalty run deep.

-draft

The voices in my head are telling me
things
That are very convincing.
The only thing is
My heart also hears it.
My mind tells me one thing
And my heart tells me another.
It's hard that they're at war with each
other,
Hopefully, my heart wins,
And hopefully, I get better.

-draft

I feel like I'm too sad to be loved,
And too broken to be fixed.
I don't like opening up
Because you see what I've been hiding.
I see one fast way to fix everything
That I'm okay with,
But my heart won't let me,
And I know others won't be okay with it.

-draft

I am someone who overthinks.
So that means I'm someone who over
loves.
Which means I'm someone who will love
you so much
That I break my own heart
Just for you.
But the sad thing is,
I'm used to breaking my own heart.
So I'll give you everything
Even if you give me nothing.

-draft

I know how to make people feel better
And happy,
By making them laugh,
But the sad thing is,
I don't know how to make myself better
And happy.
I think people think it is great to be
funny,
But in reality
Most stuff I do,
I don't really laugh at.
I'm laughing because you're laughing.
Not because I know it's funny.

-draft

Most of the time when
I'm upset with you
It's not because of what you said/did
But what you didn't say/do.
I treat you exactly how I want you to
treat me.
I say good morning to you and I stop
Say good morning to me.
I know you can't read minds
But please pay more attention to what
I'm doing
That YOU like.

8-9-20

You're a good person,
But also,
Extremely broken.
You're a softhearted person,
And you are so strong.
Be proud of that,
Because very few people
Have been able to master that skill.
And the ones that have,
Know how hard of a skill
It is to learn
And how powerful it is.

10-22-20

I've been fighting for so long
That I got used to it.
I'm afraid I'll be happy and have
someone.
I don't know how to act if I get those,
So, I don't try to get those.

-draft

All I want to do is to make people laugh
And to make them feel better.
Even if that means
Giving them my happiness.

-draft

Don't say you know me if you only know
a fraction of my life.
My own family doesn't know me that
well.
You will start to know me
When I open up to you,
And when I start to see,
Think,
And talk to you differently.

-draft

Sometimes I'll be lying in bed
Or doing something
And I just get this feeling.
It's not bad
But I say "I can die now."
Meaning that I'm satisfied with where I
am in life.
I'm not sad,
And if I die,
I won't be sad,
Because I feel like I did something right.

-draft

I've been having this internal battle for
some time.
While it was with me in the present,
It now includes my future.
What I want to be,
Who I want to be with,
Where I see myself,
Etc.

-draft

When my mother came up for Christmas
And when we were opening presents,
I felt really tired.
The magic and excitement wasn't there,
Like when I was younger.
All I could think of was what if I wasn't
here.

-draft

If this chapter of my life had a title,
It would be "The End?"
My book is being written as the day
progresses,
So the author
And reader
Don't know if it's the end
Or not.

10-31-20

Words are a powerful thing
That can make or break someone.
From giving them hope and inspiration
To killing them with their own gun.

10-31-20

If you are mad at me,
Yell at me,
Or have attitude with me,
I may think about getting mad
And think about it later,
But I'll try to stay calm.
I'll just accept it
And instead of getting mad,
I'll just get sad,
Wishing I was never here.

10-31-20

I had a dream
Where someone who I haven't seen
In a few years said to me in front of other
people
"Please don't give up."
I said a response to that.
"You don't need to worry about me,
You have your own problems to look
after,
I'll be fine,
I have a plan."
Why would my subconscious say that to
me?
Are my subconscious and mind at war
now?

12-14-20

It's hard to keep reading
And continuing on with the story
When the character you loved
Is no longer in the story.

12-14-20

I think one of the saddest things
Is when you try so hard to make yourself
happy.
You do all the things that use to make
you happy
But when you do those things
It doesn't work.
And you're sitting there thinking
About the thing you're trying to get rid
of.
It's hard and exhausting.

12-13-20

I'm not really close to my family
anymore.
We've been growing apart for some time
now.
Because of that,
They don't really know me.
They know what everybody else knows
Or they know the thing I didn't want
them to know.
They did me dirty.
Because of those
I'm awkward around them.

12-10-20

I'm telling you this
Not so you can pay attention to me,
Or to get your sympathy/empathy,
Or for your forgiveness,
But It's so you can understand.

11-9-20

Things spread.
Rumors, germs,
Cancer, viruses,
Etc.
One thing I did not expect to spread
Were my cuts.
I chose one spot because it was hidden,
But those spread,
Now anyone can see them.
It was I spot,
Now it's 9 places,
And I can't stop.

-draft

I've already accepted my fate.
I already know what's going to happen to
me in the future.
You can dislike it
And try to change it all you want,
But my fate is sealed,
And there's no changing that.

-draft

I wish my was 28-year-old self could
come
And talk to me.
Give me some advice,
Tell me when I get better,
Answer all the questions I have.
Or if he doesn't show up,
Then I know what happens.

-draft

I started back up almost 4 months ago.
I've only been able to stop for about 3
weeks.
Not all at once
But stopped for one day,
Did it again,
Stopped for one day again.
I haven't been able to go longer.
I'm sorry,
And I can't stop.

-draft

I like when it's dark outside,
Not at night
But during the day
And seeing dark clouds.
Something about it makes me whole.
Knowing that both the weather and I
Are under hard times.
I just feel better when it's dark outside.
Even better if I can hear lite rain.

11-10-20

I don't care how busy I am with work,
Papers,
Or my own problems,
If you want me to join you,
I'll put my life on hold and join you.
If I turn my paper in late,
That's on me.
I chose to join you,
And chose to do my paper late.
So don't you dare lecture me on loyalty.

-draft

Love is the one thing everybody craves.
Everyone deserves love,
But not everyone gets it.

11-11-20

Dear future wife,
I look forward to seeing you soon
And look forward to spending time with
you.
I can't wait to sing, cry, laugh,
And spend the rest of our lives together.
I pray we meet soon,
And pray you show me
That there was nothing wrong with me.
I love you
And I don't know you.

11-15-20

We see the bad things in ourselves
Because that's what we need improving
on.
After performing,
We remember everything bad about it
Because that's what we need to work on
While the audience sees what's good
about it.
We glance over what's good
Cause it doesn't need to be worked on.

11-15-20

I believe that some friends
Don't get the friend or best friend status,
But instead becomes family.

11-15-20

I don't like opening up
Because I'm afraid you will use it against
me,
See/think/talk to me differently,
See how broken I am,
Or see me how I see myself.
So I don't say anything
And only make jokes so those things
don't happen.

11-18-20

I keep telling myself to make a list
Of the little things.
Dogs, movies, games, books, laughter.
All these things that I'll miss,
Are all things that people overlook.
I wouldn't be here if not for the little
things,
And my heart.

-draft

The thing about self-harm that they
don't tell you is
That it's also an addiction.
I know self-harm, drugs, alcohol, porn
are bad,
And I want to stop,
But I just can't.
I've become addicted to it.
I'll just add it to the list of things that I
am
Or were addicted to.

-draft

I know what's wrong with me,
I can tell you everything
But we'll be here all day.
The only thing is
I can't tell you everything right with me.
I have 3 things that are good about me.
That's it.

-draft

Please be gentle with me,
I'm very fragile.
I don't trust easily
And will leave when I feel unwanted,
Annoying,
Or overstayed my welcome.
I might make jokes
But that's so you won't worry about me.

11-18-20

My story is complete,
It's done, finished.
Right now, it's just dragging on
Trying to hit a certain page length
No matter how good or bad it is.
It was finished 20 pages ago,
But the author is still writing it.
All the objectives
And story arcs are completed and done.
The author is dragging it on
To hit a page length.
That is what's going to doom this book.

-draft

I don't know what's wrong with me.
My family is complimenting me from the
other day.
And all I'm thinking of when I read those
texts are
"stop, let me leave already,
I know you don't mean it,
Just leave me alone."
Why can't I accept them,
And stop feeling this way?

-draft

I really need a hug.
I will never ask for a hug,
But I always think you'll hug me in the
back of my mind.
But the sad thing is
If you surprise hug me,
I'll just stand there
Thinking you need something from me,
Or if I slipped something serious.

-draft

I don't really like calling,
But when I do call you,
It's important
And can't be texted to you,
So please pick up.

11-23-20

I want someone who will fight for me,
And fight with me.
Who will convince me I am worthy of
love.
Who will be my motivation,
Why I don't do any more bad things.
I want someone who will love my sky
Even when it's dark and cloudy
And when my stars don't shine.

11-23-20

If I'm able to pick myself up by myself,
Then I won't really need anyone.

-draft

I wish my body
And mind were in sync with each other.
I wish my heart
And mind weren't at war with each other.
Maybe then I'd be like the old me;
Happy and joyful.

11-24-20

I've gotten so used to being mistreated,
Forgotten about,
Lack of physical touch,
And lack of love and affection,
That when I'm shown those things,
I have a panic attack
Because I'm not used to it.
While I do want to be shown those,
I know what will happen,
So I hope no one shows me it.

-draft

I hate relapsing.
Trying so hard to not do something,
Being clean for X number of days
Going all down the drain.
It sucks,
Going back to square one,
All that hard work gone.
It's like restarting a hard long game,
And you feel like giving up.
It can be drugs or it can be candy.

11-25-20

Next time you see me in person,
On the phone,
Or something else,
I will be different.
For better or for worse,
I will be different physically
And/or mentally.
Hopefully MY definition of "different"
doesn't come true.

11-25-20

I saw a quote that said
"Home is where you are loved for being
yourself."
I'm trying to find my home.
I have a key to the door
But I don't have the address.
So I'm wandering
And homeless.
Maybe when I find myself,
I'll find my home,
But that's a big maybe.

12-6-20

One thing I'm starting to get used too
Is the sound of my own voice on
recordings.
The first step in loving myself.
Despite being my own voice,
There's something soothing
And wholesome about it.
It blocks all the bad things I'm already
used to

-draft

I think the funniest people are the scariest
when angry.
Because you've never seen that side to
them.
Have you seen me angry?
It's scary.
But luckily,
I know how to control my anger.

I think the funniest people are the
saddest.
Because they make all these jokes.
Have you seen me sad?
No, I wear a mask to hide it,
And say jokes to conceal it.
But luckily,
It's easy to hide my sadness,
And you don't suspect a thing.

-draft

I'm scared to become happy.
Because I know it won't last long,
And I know my anxiety will make it
worse.
I may seem fine when you see me,
But you don't see me behind closed
doors.

-draft

I don't want kids
Because I'm afraid they'll turn out like me
And my siblings
And I don't want that.
I'm afraid I'll turn out like my parents,
My kids are going to become
Try hards, Drunks,
Losers, Stoners,
Or suicidal.
I can't deal with my kids turning out like
me
And my siblings.

-draft

Best/worst thing about wearing a mask,
I can take my other mask off.
No more faking a smile,
But sometimes my eyes,
And body language say "I'm not happy."

-draft

You see someone's true colors when
they're mad,
Drunk, or with friends.
I try to show my true colors everyday
So, if I get mad, drunk, or with friends,
I don't change on you.

-draft

Ever since I started opening up,
I've been seeing everyone differently.
When I see someone,
I always think
"They know,
Or they don't know."
And I put people into categories
Of who knows what I've been through
And who doesn't.

-draft

If I make plans with you,
I make sure it's something I can also do
by myself,
And I plan for it to be by myself.
I'm afraid you're going to cancel last
minute,
But it doesn't hurt
Cause I knew you were going to do that,
And planned for you to cancel.

-draft

2 Reasons why I do/don't want a
girlfriend.
Do: she will help me out of this well I'm
in,
She will shatter my heart and give me a
perfect opportunity.
Don't: I'm not happy by myself,
I don't want another earthly attachment.

-draft

I'm so tired.
But I'm still going to work,
Fight, stay, and do whatever I can
To not fall and to not fail.
And if I do fall,
Try my hardest to get up.
But if I don't get up,
Just know I tried my best.

12-7-20

When I say "Goodbye,"
It means we'll see each other again.
When I say "I'll See You in The Future,"
It means you're fake
And I'm just being polite,
We may see each other again
But it wasn't planned.
Or you're real,
I'll see you in heaven,
And do hope we meet again soon.

12-7-20

I've been showing the 7:20 face for some time now.
I want to change that myself by myself.

7:20 is a time on an analog clock.
If you see it,
It looks like a sad face.

-draft

It doesn't matter where you are in life,
We all have a dance with death
eventually.

-draft

I'm not afraid to let go.
I'm afraid nothing will happen,
Nothing will change,
It will be the same.
So I hold on.
And most times it hurts,
But I get used to it.

-draft

I hate but I also like
When people use my words against me.
It shows they were paying attention,
And remembered what I said.
It's me fighting myself.
They want me to take my own advice,
And it means a lot if they repeat what I say,
Word for word.

12-8-20

You can't keep reading the same chapter
of the same story.
You have to move onto the next chapter.
I know it might be hard to move on,
I know there might be some characters
that aren't going to be there,
But it's okay.
Just like the character in the story,
You too have to move on.
It's okay.

-draft

I have some poetry books.
I have these because to me it's like music;
Short,
The meanings behind them,
I can reread them,
And keeps me busy.
And I've been told the way I speak
Is very poetic,
So I read them out loud to myself.

-draft

Pay attention to what I say
And what I don't say.
I've talked about letting go,
I never said of what.
If you know me
It could be one thing,
If you don't know me
Then it could be a different thing.
Context may help,
But it's up to your interpretation
Unless you personally ask me.

-draft

Sometimes I take a while to respond to
texts
Or Snapchats.
That's because of the conversation we are
having,
How I'm feeling when I received your
text,
If I have motivation to do anything,
If we don't text often
Or Snapchat often.
When I get the notification,
My mind thinks of all these things,
So I'm scared to open
And read it,
And I have to come up with what to say.

12-15-20

The child in us never really dies.
It just gets left behind
And forgotten about by our adult self
while growing up.
If you still have the child in you,
And you are an adult,
Please don't lose
Or forget about them.

-draft

I think I knew I was starting to get better,
When I smiled and thought
"I'm glad it failed,
I'm glad I never took the perfect chance,
If it succeeded, I wouldn't be able to do
that."

12-30-20

Printed in Great Britain
by Amazon